WESTMOUNT ELEMENTARY SCHOOL
745 WALKEM ROAD
KAMLOOPS, B.C.
V2B 7Z3

Nutrition
Fit and Fats

Kristin Petrie

ABDO
Publishing Company

visit us at
www.abdopub.com

Published by ABDO Publishing Company, 4940 Viking Drive, Edina, Minnesota 55435.
Copyright © 2004 by Abdo Consulting Group, Inc. International copyrights reserved in all countries. No part of this book may be reproduced in any form without written permission from the publisher.

Printed in the United States.

Cover Photo: Corbis
Interior Photos: Corbis pp. 1, 4, 5, 6, 7, 9, 10, 12-13, 15, 17, 19, 20, 21, 23, 24, 25, 26, 27, 28

Editors: Kate A. Conley, Stephanie Hedlund, Kristianne E. Vieregger
Art Direction: Neil Klinepier

Library of Congress Cataloging-in-Publication Data

Petrie, Kristin, 1970-
   Fit and fats / Kristin Petrie.
     p. cm. -- (Nutrition)
   Includes index.
   Summary: Explains the functions of fat in a healthy diet, discussing sources of this nutrient, how the body uses fats, and what happens when too much fat is consumed.
   ISBN 1-59197-402-X
    1. Lipids in human nutrition--Juvenile literature. 2. Fat--Juvenile literature. [1. Fat. 2. Nutrition.] I. Title.

QP751.P42 2003
613.2'84--dc21

2002043624

Contents

Fats

What comes to mind when you hear or say the word *fat*? Do you say it with a smile or a grimace? Can you think of anything good to say about fat? This book will help you understand the role of fat in your diet and in your body.

Before we go on, let's get one thing straight—fat does not equal bad! Just as we need protein, carbohydrates, and water, we also need to eat some fat, just not too much. Every **nutrient** is needed in moderation and each serves a purpose.

What is a Lipid?

Lipids are organic compounds that don't dissolve in water. The word *fat* is commonly used for all lipids. Fats, however, are actually solid lipids. Oils, on the other hand, are liquid lipids at room temperature.

So, what is the purpose of fat in your body? You probably already know that body fat keeps you warm on cold days. However, did you also know that it keeps you, and your **organs**, cool when it's hot outside? And, when a ball hits you in the chest, remember that fat cushions the blow to your organs.

Oil is a liquid lipid.

Catching a ball seems harmless. But, if you didn't have enough fat, the force of the ball would injure your organs. They need a cushion of fat to protect them.

Food Sources of Fat

It is easy to think of foods that are rich in fat. Ice cream, French fries, and butter are foods high in saturated fats. Eating these fats in large amounts is unhealthy. Saturated fats contribute to health problems, such as heart disease and **cancer**.

On the other hand, unsaturated fats are healthy. Unsaturated fats are found in foods that come from plants. Examples of these foods are olives, peanuts, and walnuts. Unsaturated fats help lower blood cholesterol and the risk of heart disease.

French fries and ice cream are foods high in unhealthy saturated fats.

Meats and other sources of protein are also high in saturated fats.

Fat's Jobs in the Body

In the body, fats are part of every cell, **organ**, and **tissue**. The fat under your skin is like a protective blanket that wraps around you. It shields your bones and tissues from damage and from hot and cold temperatures.

Fat does other jobs in your body, too. Deposits of fat surround, cushion, and hold in place organs such as your heart and kidneys. Fat also keeps cell **membranes** strong. This protects cells against attack by germs or damage by chemicals.

Fat also has the job of aiding vitamins. The vitamins A, D, E, and K need fat to help them travel in blood. Fat not only helps move these vitamins around, it also helps them absorb into cells. Without fat, these vitamins would just go in one end and out the other!

Fat helps keep you warm when it's cold!

Possibly the most important task that fat performs is to give you a huge supply of energy. Fat allows you to keep playing, even when you are too busy to stop and "refuel." Fat provides more than twice the amount of energy per gram than either protein or carbohydrates.

Fat is providing energy, warmth, and cell protection to these children while they play.

For example, if a lima bean weighed one gram and were made of pure fat, it would give you nine calories of energy. But, if that lima bean were instead made of pure protein or carbohydrates, it would only give you four calories of energy. As you can see, this makes fat very concentrated in calories and energy.

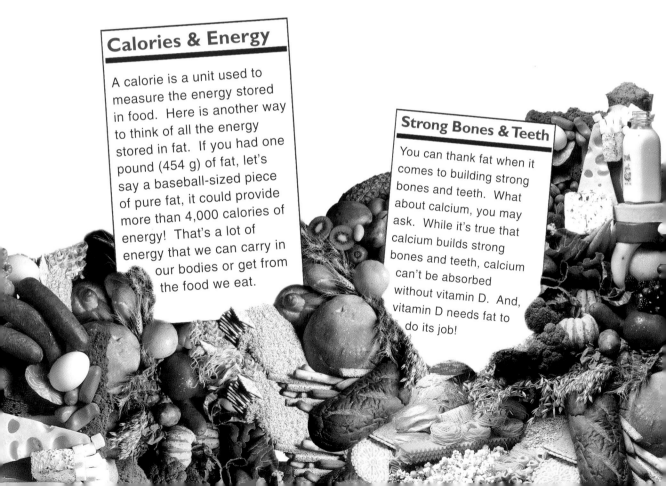

Calories & Energy

A calorie is a unit used to measure the energy stored in food. Here is another way to think of all the energy stored in fat. If you had one pound (454 g) of fat, let's say a baseball-sized piece of pure fat, it could provide more than 4,000 calories of energy! That's a lot of energy that we can carry in our bodies or get from the food we eat.

Strong Bones & Teeth

You can thank fat when it comes to building strong bones and teeth. What about calcium, you may ask. While it's true that calcium builds strong bones and teeth, calcium can't be absorbed without vitamin D. And, vitamin D needs fat to do its job!

Fat's Role in Foods

Fat also plays important roles in the foods we eat. One role is to give many foods a pleasing taste and texture. Ice cream, for example, is smooth and creamy partly because of its high fat content. Sherbet, on the other hand, has a very different feel and taste. It is icy and sugary because it has very little fat.

Fat & Nutrients

One cup of whole milk has 150 calories. But, one cup of skim milk has only 86 calories. Why? The fat was removed in the skim milk, but no other nutrients were taken away. Likewise, one small baked potato has around 100 calories. The same baked potato, fried into French fries, has about twice as many calories, but no additional nutritional value.

Fat also carries the scent of many foods. Think of bacon or other meats cooking—they have a very distinct scent. Another function of fat in foods is its ability to make you feel full. This is called satiety. A hamburger, for example, will make you feel fuller than a bowl of rice, which has little fat.

Another role of fat, of course, is to provide calories. You read earlier that fat is a big supplier of energy to your body. So, fat in food is a concentrated source of calories. The high calorie and energy content is part of the reason that fat gets a bad rap.

Fatty Acids

So far, you have learned about fat and why you need it to survive. But, did you know that there are several different types of fat? They are all made from fatty acids.

What exactly are fatty acids? They are not nearly as scary as they sound! Fatty acids are the building blocks of fats. If we break down these fatty acids, we are left with the **elements** carbon, hydrogen, and oxygen.

There are two main types of fatty acids. Some are called saturated, and some are called unsaturated. We can tell them apart by looking at how many carbon and hydrogen molecules they have.

If each carbon of a fatty acid has a hydrogen molecule attached to it, it is called a saturated fatty acid. Saturated fatty acids are usually solid at room temperature. They are found in foods that come from animals, such as meat, milk, and cheese. A few plant oils, such as palm oil and coconut oil, are also saturated fatty acids.

This boy's clothing is saturated. That's because every inch of his clothing has water attached to it.

16

On the other hand, if some of the carbons on the fatty acid do not have hydrogen, it is called an unsaturated fatty acid. They come from vegetable oils and fish. Unsaturated fatty acids are usually in a liquid form.

The body makes most of the fatty acids it needs from other **nutrients**. Some fatty acids, however, the body cannot make. For this reason, they are called essential fatty acids (EFAs). Usually, you receive EFAs from your foods—such as seeds, nuts, and corn—without even knowing it.

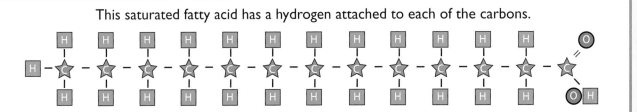

H Hydrogen ☆ Carbon ⊙ Oxygen

This saturated fatty acid has a hydrogen attached to each of the carbons.

This monounsaturated fatty acid is missing hydrogen on one pair of carbons.

This polyunsaturated fatty acid is missing hydrogen on more than one pair of carbons.

EFAs are in this ear of corn. That makes it nutritious as well as delicious!

Unsaturated Fatty Acids

There are two types of unsaturated fatty acids. Monounsaturated fatty acids are missing one set of hydrogen molecules. Polyunsaturated fatty acids are missing more than one set of hydrogen molecules. An easy way to remember this is to know that *mono* means one, and *poly* means many.

Cholesterol

Cholesterol is a fat made by your body. It is also found in foods such as eggs and meat. Cholesterol has many important jobs, such as making and maintaining cell **membranes**. It also protects cells and nervous **tissues**. Nervous tissues send signals to your body, such as to move your arm or twitch your eye. This important fat aids in making **hormones**. And, it helps form **bile salts**, which assist your body in **digesting** food.

Cholesterol has been blamed for clogging arteries. Dietary cholesterol, however, is not really the bad guy. The total amount of saturated fat in your diet combined with your **genetic** information is what causes fat to build up in your arteries. This is yet another reason to eat fat, especially the saturated kind, in moderation.

Types of Lipoproteins

Lipoproteins are compounds of fat and protein. Lipoproteins that have more fat than protein are called low-density lipoproteins (LDLs). Lipoproteins that have more protein than fat are called high-density lipoproteins (HDLs).

You have probably also heard of good and bad cholesterol. High-density **lipoproteins** (HDLs) are good. HDLs have the ability to take cholesterol in the blood and return it to the liver. This prevents cholesterol from building up in the arteries. People with high HDL levels have less risk of heart disease. That's because their cholesterol is cleared from the blood faster.

Low-density lipoproteins (LDLs) are bad. LDLs hold a lot of cholesterol. And, unfortunately, they have the bad habit of hanging out and clogging up the arteries. This makes it difficult for blood to flow to and from the heart.

Cholesterol protects cells and nervous tissues. Healthy cells and nervous tissues allow these children to wave.

Hydrogenation

A process called hydrogenation was invented to make unsaturated, liquid fat into saturated, solid fat. It is used in products such as peanut butter. Normally, the fat that comes out of peanuts is unsaturated. So, it floats to the top of a jar of peanut butter. However, most people like their peanut butter without that oil at the top. So, manufacturers use hydrogenation to keep the fat mixed into the peanut butter.

Hydrogenation has benefits. It makes some foods, such as peanut butter, more appealing. It also makes some foods last longer. However, hydrogenation has its downsides, too. For example, it makes the fat less healthy for your heart.

Eating a little peanut butter is not bad for your health! Like any other high-fat food, however, too much makes for an unbalanced diet.

Digestion

What happens to fat after you eat it? Let's follow the path of one of the most common forms of fat, triglyceride. It is made up of one molecule of glycerol with three fatty acids attached. When triglycerides are bound to one another in a chain, voilà— they form a fat!

In **digestion**, the chain of triglycerides breaks. This happens when it reaches the small intestine. There, the triglycerides are mixed with **bile salts** from the gallbladder. These strong salts break the fat into several smaller molecules called micelles.

A Triglyceride

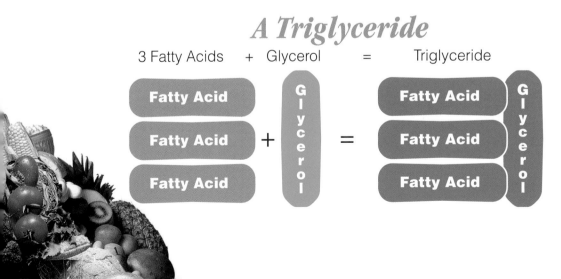

3 Fatty Acids   +   Glycerol   =   Triglyceride

*These skaters show the first step of fat digestion.
They started as a chain but will soon separate.*

Next, **enzymes** from the pancreas attack the micelles. They are further broken down into individual fatty acids and glycerol. These small pieces are now able to pass through the surface of your small intestine and into its cells.

But we're not done yet! In the intestine's cells, the glycerol and fatty acids are put back together. Then, the rebuilt triglycerides are coated with a protein. This allows them to be carried around in the body and delivered to where they are needed. First they are delivered to the **lymphatic system**, then to the bloodstream.

A solid fat has to break apart in order to pass through the cell wall. On the other side, fat will be rebuilt to do its job just as these blocks will be rebuilt into a new tower.

Whew! That was complicated. You might be wondering why fat molecules break down if they're just going to be rebuilt. Fat molecules are too big to cross cell **membranes**! They have to be broken apart so they will fit through the walls of the intestines and other cells. Once they manage to get through the cell's small openings, they like to get back together and travel around the body as larger molecules.

Fat Digestion & Rebuilding

1. Small Intestine
   Triglyceride chains are broken down.

2. Gallbladder
   Bile salts from the gallbladder break fats into micelles in the intestines.

3. Pancreas
   Enzymes from the pancreas break micelles apart, and pieces pass into intestine cell walls and then into the lymphatic system and bloodstream.

Requirements

There is no specific recommended daily allowance for dietary fats. You could actually live on very little fat. Because fat is found in so many protein- and carbohydrate-rich foods, meeting your body's needs is very easy.

Fat should be around one-third of your total calories. However, this is difficult to understand since we don't usually eat a stick of butter or other foods that are pure fat! Basically, think before you eat. Do your best to limit foods that have lots of fat but little else to offer. You don't want to fill your body with unhealthy fat and empty calories. After all, you need the good stuff to build and replenish your growing body.

Remember, staying fit starts with watching your fat intake. When you don't use the fat, it is stored for later use. Too much stored fat will cause you to gain weight. And, then it is hard to stay healthy.

Exercise and eat right to stay fit!

The fat around this piece of meat is an example of a lipid at room temperature.

Schools work hard to provide children with a balanced diet. School lunches are low in fat and should contain a serving from each of the food groups.

Too Much Fat

In the United States, many people eat much more fat than their bodies need. Unfortunately, much of this is the unhealthy type—saturated fat. As you already know, many diseases such as **cancer**, heart disease, and obesity are linked to this problem.

This plate has very little fat on it. It is a good example of a balanced meal that includes grains, vegetables, and meat.

For these reasons, it is wise, even at a young age, to pay attention to the type and amount of fat you are eating. Some ways to be sure that you are limiting your overall fat and saturated fat intake are listed below.

 • Choose low-fat protein sources, such as fish, turkey, chicken, and legumes.

 • When eating meats, choose lower-fat or lean types and cut off excess fat.

 • Use skim and low-fat milk products instead of whole-fat dairy foods.

 • Choose broiled, baked, or boiled foods more often than fried foods.

 • Include lots of fruits, vegetables, and whole grains in your diet. These foods have very little or no saturated fat.

Glossary

bile salt - a crystal made by your liver and stored in your gallbladder. Bile salt mixes with fats in your small intestine and breaks them into smaller molecules.

cancer - any of a group of often deadly diseases characterized by an abnormal growth of cells that destroys healthy tissues and organs.

digest - to break down food into substances small enough for the body to absorb.

element - one of more than 100 basic substances from which all other things are made.

enzyme - a complex protein produced in the living cells of all plants and animals. It is used in many of the body's functions, from digestion to clotting.

genetic - of or relating to the branch of biology that deals with the principles of heredity.

hormones - chemical messengers that help regulate activities in the body.

lipoprotein - a chemical compound made of fat and protein. Lipoproteins are found in the blood, where their main function is to carry cholesterol.

lymphatic system - a system that transports a fluid called lymph. Lymph bathes the body's cells, bringing them nourishment and oxygen and taking away waste.

membrane - the outer layer or "skin" of a cell.

nutrient - a substance found in food and used in the body to promote growth, maintenance, and repair.

organ - a part of an animal or plant that is composed of several kinds of tissues and that performs a specific function. The heart, liver, gallbladder, and intestines are organs of an animal.

tissue - a group or cluster of similar cells that work together, such as a muscle.

Saying It

cholesterol - kuh-LES-tuh-rohl
enzyme - EN-zime
genetic - juh-NEH-tihk
glycerol - GLIH-suh-rawl
hydrogenation - hi-drah-juh-NAY-shuhn
lipoprotein - lip-oh-PROH-teen

lymphatic - lihm-FAH-tihk
micelle - my-SEHL
obesity - oh-BEE-suh-tee
satiety - suh-TI-uh-tee
saturated - SAH-chuh-ray-tuhd
triglyceride - tri-GLIH-suh-ride

Web Sites

To learn more about the nutrient fat, visit ABDO Publishing Company on the World Wide Web at **www.abdopub.com**. Web sites about fats and fitness are featured on our Book Links page. These links are routinely monitored and updated to provide the most current information available.

Index